Conflict Resolution Training for the Classroom

Conflict Resolution Training for the Classroom

What Every ESL Teacher Needs to Know

By

Barrie J. Roberts

University of Michigan Press
Ann Arbor

First paperback edition 2023

Published in the United States of America by the
University of Michigan Press

Paperback ISBN: 978-0-472-03955-5
Ebook ISBN: 978-0-472-12687-3

First published January 2020

ACKNOWLEDGMENTS

This book would not have been possible without the vision and guidance of my editor, Kelly Sippell, and my UC–Berkeley colleagues and friends: Margi Wald, Maggie Sokolik, Sybil Marcus, Melody Noll, Michael Clark, and Jen Burton—with special appreciation to Melody, my longtime Mediation as a Second Language partner. Most of all, I am grateful to the authors of *Getting to Yes*, William Ury and Bruce Patton, who generously encouraged my vision of using their book to teach ESL worldwide. Because of their book, so many ESL students have found their deepest aspirations for themselves and the world expressed in an English they can understand, with a little help from their ESL instructors.

ABOUT THE AUTHOR

Barrie J. Roberts has been a public interest lawyer, mediator, ESL instructor, and Alternative Dispute Resolution (ADR) Administrator for two Southern California Superior Courts, working with judges, court staff, lawyers, and mediators to develop court-connected settlement programs.

She created the term **Mediation as a Second Language** (**MSL**) to teach English through negotiation and mediation, and has taught variations of the MSL material at UC–Berkeley and Chapman University's Fowler School of Law in Orange, California. To encourage ESL instructors to create their own versions of MSL, she has given teacher training workshops at UC–Berkeley, TESOL, CATESOL, ETAI, the Global Legal Skills Conference, the Joint International Conference on ESP in Asia, and the Global Negotiation Symposium (GNS) at Kobe City University of Foreign Studies. She has also served as a judge at the Intercollegiate Negotiation Competition in Tokyo.

In addition to MSL, she has taught a wide range of ESL courses and levels including beginning adult education, TOEFL® prep, legal English, business English, human rights, public speaking, academic reading and writing, speaking and listening, academic skills, and American humor.

After obtaining a BA in political science from UC–Berkeley, she received her JD from UC–Hastings College of the Law, an MA in TESOL from CSU Sacramento, and an LLM in Dispute Resolution from the Pepperdine University School of Law, Straus Institute.

CONTENTS

Introduction

Who Is This Book For?

This book is for ESL instructors without any background in conflict resolution (CR) who teach intermediate to advanced ESL courses in college, university, graduate programs, and Intensive English Programs (IEPs). Whether your focus is language or content or both, this book will help you find your own special blend so that you can provide your students with valuable negotiation and mediation skills along with their English.

ESL instructors in many other contexts, from kindergarten to adult education, can also use the ideas in this book to integrate CR into their language lessons. I hope this book will also be useful to ESL instructors with a great deal of CR experience who may be teaching EAP and ESP courses in business, law, social justice, or peace studies. Finally, I hope this book will contribute to Peace Linguistics, a field I was excited to learn about while writing this book.

Terms Used in This Book

- **ESL:** Teachers may be in a variety of settings worldwide—ESL (English as a Second Language), EFL (English as a Foreign Language), EAL (English as an Additional Language), EAP (English for Academic Purposes), ESP (English for Specific Purposes), or in bilingual programs. This book will use ESL as shorthand for all of these teaching contexts.
- **CR** is the abbreviation for **conflict resolution**. This is an umbrella term for a variety of communication processes including negotiation and mediation. As we will see, CR also includes tools for working with others to *prevent* conflict and promote positive relationships in many different situations.
- This book uses two terms interchangeably to describe the overall approach to combining ESL and CR: **Mediation as a Second Language (MSL)** and **Conflict Resolution for ESL (CRESL).**

- **Principled negotiation** is the system we use for CRESL training. Developed at the Harvard Negotiation Project, this common-sense approach to getting our needs met while protecting our relationships is fully described, step by step, in *Getting to Yes* (Fisher et al., 2011). First published in 1983, this book was written for a popular audience but is also taught in business, law, and international relations programs worldwide, and it is my main text for CRESL courses.
- **Active listening** is CRESL's main communication tool for principled negotiation and other CR purposes. The active listener's twin goals are to fully understand the speaker and to demonstrate that understanding (or sincere efforts to develop it) through skillful, non-judgmental questions and responses. "Understanding is not agreeing" (Fisher et al., 2011, p. 37), however, a key point for CR.

Introduction to CRESL

My basic lesson plan looks like this: students choose a conflict that is meaningful to them and then create a role-play to resolve it. Of course, there is a little more to it. We prepare for the role-plays with ESL and CR activities, and after the role-plays we reflect on what did and did not work. But that is it in a nutshell.

Assuming that you would like to try this lesson plan after you have prepared by using the material in this ebook, what types of conflicts would your students choose? My students have chosen personal conflicts with parents, romantic partners, roommates, professors, landlords, and tour operators; fictional conflicts from literature and movies; conflicts they have studied in history, business, law, and other courses; social justice conflicts in the daily news and on campus; and intractable global conflicts among nations. After making their selections, my diverse students have huddled together in small groups to negotiate or mediate creative yet practical win-win solutions for all of these types of conflicts using the frameworks and charts provided in this ebook. Additionally, throughout the course and after the course ends, students share stories about how they have applied their new CR communication tools, sometimes translated into their first languages, to real-life problems.

I will share more specific examples later, but first, you might be wondering how CRESL developed. I started experimenting with CR in my ESL courses after a few light-bulb moments in a community mediation course that had nothing to do with ESL. During a beginning partner exercise, the As told their stories about a scary childhood experience to the Bs, who listened and "repeated back," according to the mediation trainer's specific instructions. It suddenly occurred to me that this simple, active listening exercise would be an engaging communication activity for my ESL students.

That bubble burst exactly one moment later when I realized that beginning active listening for CR was just a routine "paraphrase and check" exercise for ESL. But why did the same exercise work so well for two completely different fields? What do CR and ESL have to do with each other? As I thought about how both CR and ESL focus on language and aim to improve understanding, communication, and critical thinking, **Mediation as a Second Language** (**MSL**) popped into my head.

Curious as to whether these light-bulb moments would burn out or burn on, I started revising a few of the CR activities I had just learned as a mediation student for the ESL students I was teaching. At first, I just added relevant vocabulary and grammar points to some easy CR activities, with backup plans in case things did not go well. But things went very well right from the start. During CR activities, students use English for the authentic purpose of learning practical CR communication skills. They can immediately apply these new skills to academic purposes (e.g., improving group discussions, group projects, email, office hours) and to daily life on and off campus (e.g., roommates, relatives, romantic interests). And, during class, learning takes place more through interactive exercises and role-plays than from listening to the sage on the stage. Language is learned as needed to prepare for a role-play or during on-the-spot teachable moments during an activity, but not because it is in the next chapter in the textbook. Best of all, once students (and instructors) learn fundamental CR principles and skills, they can apply them to many academic, professional, and personal purposes.

Here are some examples of such applications from my CRESL classes:

1. In an intermediate-level ESL academic writing course at a community college, an East European student confidently approached the blackboard and used a chart (see Figure 3.2) to demonstrate how World War I could have been prevented. To explain "what could have been," she focused on conditionals and verb tenses (*If Britain and Italy had intervened earlier, then....*).
2. In a high-intermediate multi-skills course, an Italian student mediated a dispute between his Korean and Japanese classmates concerning the depiction of Korea in Japanese textbooks. He skillfully used modals and the passive voice to promote brainstorming (*How*

could the facts have been told in other ways?) and new idioms (*Looks like you BOTH have steam coming out of your ears!*) to promote bonding and a touch of humor, resulting in several joint proposals for textbook revisions.

3. During an emergency mediation between the Capulets and Montagues, six high-intermediate international students, all Chinese and Korean science or computer science majors, used their new group discussion and pronunciation skills to prevent a tragedy: *I'd like to ask BOTH families to respond to THIS question: You are BOTH hoping for GRANDCHILDREN to expand your POWER, am I RIGHT?* Romeo and Juliet's descendants are still in Verona, living happily ever after.
4. A trip to Yosemite is a popular weekend activity for UC–Berkeley international students, but unfortunately, tour operators do not always deliver what they promise. One operator was surprised to be on the receiving end of the assertive communication skills my intermediate Chinese IEP students had practiced in class, and after a disappointing trip, they negotiated a 50 percent refund.
5. One summer, a Chinese couple decided to take a CRESL course together but had to enroll in different sections due to scheduling. All summer long, my colleague Melody Noll and I read journal entries describing each side's version of their various squabbles and how, just when things looked hopeless, they suddenly remembered to try something from class to seek a win-win solution. Inspired by their experience, I proposed a new course, "CRESL for Couples," but have not heard back.
6. Long before Saudi Arabia allowed women to drive, my male and female Saudi LLM students, all with law degrees from Saudi Arabia and a range of English skills, chose to conduct a negotiation on that topic. To my surprise, instead of focusing on women's rights, they used their new brainstorming and problem-solving skills to work out solutions to routine logistical challenges, such as training female police officers and driving instructors, so that progress could be made without threatening shared cultural values.
7. In my academic reading and writing course, an advanced-level UC–Berkeley student from Mexico was able to use her new critical-thinking skills to reflect on her ongoing arguments with dorm-mates over "choice vs. life." While preparing for the exercise in which she would have to stand in the shoes of the other side, she was surprised to identify several values she shared with those on the other side,

such as concern for the health and well-being of women and children and opposition to the death penalty. She had never thought about those holding the opposite view in this way, and now she had some new ideas about how she could share her views in ways that her friends on the other side could understand and respect, starting with her word choices. She hoped to work with these friends to create joint projects based on empathy to make abortion preventable and rare.

I hope these examples show how integrating CR and ESL gives students practical CR skills while simultaneously improving their English, critical-thinking, collaboration, participation, cross-cultural communication, and leadership skills. For an even wider range of applications, see Chapter 4, "CRESL Applications."

But what about your students?

1. Would the basic lesson plan (choose a meaningful conflict and work together to resolve it) work for them?
2. On a scale of 1–10 (1 = asleep at their desks; 10 = the bell rings but nobody's leaving), how would you rate their expected level of interest?
3. How would you rate this activity's benefits to your students' developing language, academic, professional, and life skills?
4. How would you rate your personal level of satisfaction as you watch your students work together to negotiate resolutions to meaningful conflicts, in English, with the language and CR skills you have provided?

In my 15-plus years of experience with this type of activity in a variety of teaching contexts, from IEP to LLM, my scale usually reaches 10 on all of these questions. I wrote this ebook to inspire you to try CR too and to help you achieve similar results with simple try-it-on-Monday activities, with syllabi for whole courses, or with lessons and activities in between.

How to Use This Book

Perhaps the examples from my CRESL classes are inspiring but also a bit intimidating. If so, here are four common concerns that ESL instructors have shared about using CR in their classrooms followed by suggestions about how to use this ebook to resolve them.

1. **How could I ever learn enough about CR to guide my students through such a wide variety of topics?** Once you learn the CR basics in Chapter 1, "Introduction to Conflict Resolution," you will be able to apply them to almost any conflict, from personal to political. If you would like to learn more about CR, take a look at the user-friendly options in Appendix A.
2. **How could I ever find the time to create new CR lessons for my ESL students?** You do not have to create any lessons to start teaching CRESL. First, you may be able to use or tweak your current ESL lessons because, whether you know it or not, if you are teaching ESL, you are already teaching the fundamentals of CR. This is the subject of Chapter 2, "Conflict Resolution and ESL." Second, this ebook provides a variety of activities that should feel familiar and doable in Chapter 3, "Sample CRESL Activities." After a semester of engaging in these integrated ESL and CR activities, one of my students described his CRESL course as "two for the price of one."
3. **How could I ever find the time to add CR to my demanding syllabi and daily lesson plans?** I promise that the purpose of this ebook is not to try to convince you to add a lot of new things to your teaching schedule. Instead, the goal is to show how, with some rethinking about what you are already doing, you could be giving your students valuable negotiation and mediation skills while covering the ESL and academic skills you have to cover. My student's "two for the price of one" remark was apt but does not go far enough: CRESL activities can serve multiple purposes in one fell swoop, as described in the next section. Rather than taking up extra class time, a focus on CRESL for a few lessons or as a course theme could instead help you cover all that you have to cover even more efficiently.
4. **What could go wrong?** Perhaps you wonder what you would do if a CR activity did not work. What if the students cannot reach an agreement? What if they get stuck and no one knows what to do? What if they get into a fight rather than resolve one? What if you try to apply a CR activity to classroom management and it does not seem to work?

I think you will be able to answer these questions for yourself after reading this ebook, but answers to frequently asked questions like these are provided in Appendix B.

How Can CR Training Benefit My Students?

CR training provides the soft communication skills that students need to succeed at school, on the job, and in their personal lives. By simultaneously providing the language and cultural skills needed to deploy these soft skills in English, CRESL activities benefit students in these important ways:

1. **Language:** Learning English through CR content and communication skills provides students with meaningful and authentic opportunities to improve their accuracy, fluency, and confidence. My students have remarked that they enjoyed "studying English without studying English" during in-class role-plays and out-of-class conflict prevention and resolution activities (i.e., homework).
2. **Academic skills for ESL and non-ESL courses:** CR training provides specific skills in communication, critical thinking, empathy, collegiality, and social graces that help students improve their participation in class and small-group discussions, group projects, meetings during office hours, and appropriate online communications. The integrated CR/ESL approach provides the English language and cultural skills our students need to accomplish all of these things.
3. **Online communication skills:** If you are engaged in technology-based ESL activities, note that **online dispute resolution** (**ODR**) (using video-conferencing, text, chat, and algorithm-based software programs to resolve disputes) is becoming an essential part of CR in legal, business, diplomatic, and other contexts, which could synchronize well with online and tech-based activities in—and beyond—the ESL classroom.
4. **Life skills:** Integrated CR and ESL training gives ESL students practical tools to deal with such distracting problems as culture shock, roommates, landlords, school administrators, visas, work, family, and, of course, romance. It also provides tools to analyze and address complex and controversial social justice and political disputes both in and out of the classroom. And long after students leave our classrooms, this training will have prepared them to become cultural bridges and global citizens for years to come.
5. **Professional skills:** CR training helps to improve professional and workplace communication skills in general, but for law, business,

diplomacy, social work, and similar professions, CR is a key component of the day-to-day work: negotiation can be a required job skill. For ESL students in these fields, negotiation and mediation courses for native speakers can be extremely challenging due to fast-paced role-plays, idioms, cultural references and assumptions (including variations in business and legal culture), body language, and sociolinguistics (e.g., apologies, tone, direct/indirect communication styles). These points can be taught and practiced when CRESL is taught as ESP for Negotiation or Mediation, but such courses can be hard to find. Providing this instruction and practice even for general ESL purposes will benefit students who need but cannot find such courses, as well as students who are preparing for professional careers in just about any field.

How Can CR Training Benefit ESL Instructors?

As wise people have been saying for hundreds of years, and as many of us know from our own experience, one of the best ways to learn something is to teach it. Learning about CR in order to teach it can benefit ESL instructors in these ways:

1. Learning how to prevent and resolve conflict with basic negotiation and mediation skills can benefit and empower us professionally and personally.
2. Teaching integrated lessons in CR/ESL is satisfying and enjoyable, with limitless opportunities for creative applications to language, content, and skills in—and beyond—the classroom.
3. Although classroom management is not this book's purpose, CR training gives instructors and students a common language and set of tools to deal with classroom issues, from tardy arrivals to group projects to plagiarism.

Goals and Warnings

When we provide CR training in our ESL classrooms, our goal is to show students how to use their English language skills to prevent and resolve conflict. This ebook describes one approach, based on principled negotiation, but there are other effective ways as well, including approaches from our students' cultures and countries.

The purpose of CRESL is for everyone, teachers and students alike, to develop our own ways to deal with conflict by improving our understanding, empathy, and communication skills, and we are all continually learning from each other.

Thus, if students challenge CR as we present it, or offer alternative approaches from their personal or cultural backgrounds, our attitude should be positive, curious, encouraging, and, in my case, thrilled. For ESL purposes, these challenges show that students are engaged, empowered, thinking critically, and using English for authentic purposes. For CR purposes, we have the opportunity to learn something new about cross-cultural communication or negotiation. Let's not conflate our preferred CR processes with our ultimate CR goals. After all, depending on the circumstances, our approach may not always be the most effective option.

However, when teaching CR, we have to start somewhere, with some sort of approach and framework. Students may criticize principled negotiation from the rooftops, but they should still try to understand and use it, as is, for these empowering reasons:

1. **Focus on CR:** Principled negotiation may be used on them in their personal and professional lives, so they need to be able to respond to it appropriately. This approach may turn out to be the best one to use with partners and adversaries from other cultures.
2. **Focus on critical thinking:** Students are asked to try this approach, not believe in it. For critical-thinking purposes, students may note their challenges to the process, request permission to try alternative approaches, and then report back to you or the whole class on the strengths and weaknesses of the various approaches.
3. **Focus on language:** CR is a great, natural way to improve English language skills.

1. Introduction to Conflict Resolution

This section is a user-friendly introduction to conflict resolution (CR) for ESL instructors interested in using CR to enrich their ESL lessons. While it does not fully prepare students for real-life negotiations and mediations outside the classroom, it does prepare ESL instructors for the activities in Chapters 3, "Sample CRESL Activities" and 4, "CRESL Applications."

CR Concepts in a Nutshell

As explained earlier, CR is an umbrella term for a variety of ways to prevent and resolve conflicts. The term is also used as shorthand for the two main methods of CR, **negotiation** and **mediation.**

Negotiation

In negotiation, we try to get what we want by reaching an agreement or understanding with another person. Whether we negotiate on our own, or an attorney or agent negotiates on our behalf, the key feature of negotiation, as shown in Figure 1.1, is the direct communication between the two sides, with no judge, referee, mediator, or other third person to buffer, assist, or decide who wins.

Negotiation is an activity that should be familiar to teachers and students alike. Think about it: how many times have you worked things out with others in the last 24 hours? But think about this as well: how did you negotiate? Did you have a system or did you just muddle through? Were you so focused on the relationship that you gave up on what you really needed? Or were you so focused on what you wanted that you risked the relationship to get it? Instead of being too accommodating or too competitive, did you try to avoid dealing

Figure 1.1 Representation of Negotiation

with the issue altogether, hoping that things would just work out without blowing up?

These are examples of traditional negotiation strategies that people use when they lack a system and set of skills to get what they need while protecting their relationships, which, as discussed earlier, is **principled negotiation** in a nutshell (Fisher et al., 2011). In real life, we have to be prepared to respond to a range of negotiation skills and tactics, including *arguing, debating, manipulating,* and *haggling.* In CRESL classrooms, however, we use more effective strategies, including communication strategies that should feel familiar to most ESL instructors.

Instead of working against each other to create winners, losers, and bad feelings, principled negotiation requires us to work together as partners to solve a problem in ways that work for all concerned. For CRESL purposes, the "problem" is going to be that two or more people with different interests have to either work something out (e.g., the sale of a house or car, an itinerary, sharing an apartment or office, who gets the last seat in a lifeboat), or resolve a strong disagreement or conflict. In both cases, resolution may seem impossible at first, especially when one side demands black and the other demands white, unless they agree to compromise and settle for gray.

But seeking a quick compromise based on what each party demands is not the goal of principled negotiation. Principled negotiators know that there is much more to the story than meets the eye and that seeking solutions comes toward the end, not the beginning of any negotiation. Principled negotiators know that "information is power" and that their first job is to find out what is really going on: why have the parties staked out these positions? Why is this deal or conflict so significant to each person? Which "needs" (Maslow, 1943) and emotions are being triggered? Do the parties share the same understanding of the situation? Have there been misunderstandings based on poor communication skills? Do they share any needs? Will each party achieve a better result by working together, agreeing to go their separate ways, or calling on others to participate in the discussion? After exploring these and other questions, there are usually many more options for an amicable and sustainable resolution than seemed possible at the start. But how do we get the answers to these questions?

Aside from internet searches, negotiators acquire the puzzle pieces they need in order to gain a full understanding of the situation by skillfully asking each other for the missing information through active listening (discussed in Chapters 2, "Conflict Resolution and ESL" and 3, "Sample CRESL Activities"). If you use jigsaw activities, you can think of negotiation as an information gap exercise in which students use active listening—and their intense curiosity—to work together to fill in the holes about each other's perspectives so they can create a win-win solution.

We can also picture principled negotiation as a journey. The journey starts in a harsh environment with the one-sided facts and demands each party presents before embarking on their negotiation. As they learn how to use active listening to communicate with each other about what is really going on, the parties end up in a lush environment that promotes empathy and problem-solving. In this setting, the former adversaries are now eager to work together as partners to "crack the case" by identifying solutions that meet their needs instead of their initial demands.

With practice, principled negotiation becomes a simple but effective way to talk with each other about what is important to us. CRESL students naturally start using principled negotiation with each other informally to discuss personal problems they are experiencing. But the very same principles and strategies are used in formal settings as well. I once worked with a Superior Court judge who, in the spirit of principled negotiation, regularly ordered lawyers out to the hallway to have one last "conversation" to see if a trial, which would produce a winner and a loser, was really in each side's best interests, or if the lawyers could do a better job for their clients just by talking with each other about what their clients really needed.

For a sample negotiation format for CRESL role-plays, see Chapter 3, "Sample CRESL Activities."

Mediation

The key feature of mediation is the third person. Throughout history and the world, various cultures have used third parties to help others resolve disputes. In some cultures, the mediator serves as a go-between or advocate, trying to bring about a desired result to benefit a family, community, or society in general. However, in the United States, and for CRESL purposes, we generally expect mediators to be 100 percent neutral, to have no stake in the outcome, and to allow the individual parties to reach their own decisions.

As the California Evidence Code puts it, mediation is "a process in which neutral persons facilitate communication between the disputants to assist them in reaching a mutually acceptable agreement" that they create for themselves [Section 1115(a)]. Figure 1.2 shows why we, along with the Evidence Code, can think of mediators as people who help others negotiate between themselves.

Mediators may use a range of tools and approaches. Some keep all the parties together in the same room from start to finish; others spend the whole

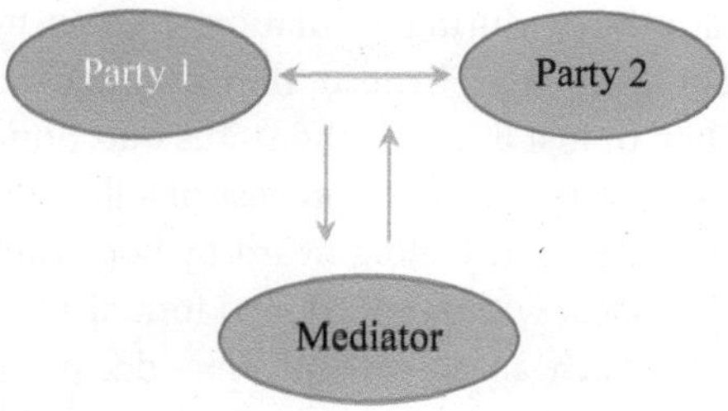

Figure 1.2 Mediation

mediation shuttling between parties in separate rooms. Some mediators take a directive approach, strongly encouraging resolution; others take a "less is more" approach, gently encouraging the parties to seek understanding rather than focusing on a settlement agreement.

Nevertheless, there are some commonalities. For most purposes, including CRESL, mediators do not decide the outcome, force parties to agree, or even provide solutions unless the parties ask for their ideas. If the parties do not want to go to court but still want a neutral third person to decide what should be done, they should seek *arbitration*, a topic that is beyond the scope of this book.

In the approach we use for CRESL, the parties should be doing most of the talking. This approach promotes both CR and language learning, and for the student mediators, leadership training as well. First, the parties speak directly to the mediators, who respond with active listening, and then they speak with each other, with the help of the mediators. Sometimes the mediator does not even have to say a word.

After my very first courthouse mediation, the opposing attorneys complimented me for helping them resolve a bitter case—by staying out of their way. After several years of costly and emotional litigation, these attorneys were suddenly facing an open courtroom with a judge waiting for them. The ticking clock and the morning sunlight from that courtroom window must have penetrated their bluster because they finally agreed to meet with a mediator. Decked out in my new suit, fresh yellow legal pad in hand, I had just started squeaking out my well-prepared mediator's "opening statement" when one attorney announced that he had an idea. With more relief than I hope I showed, I stopped talking and they settled their case. They thanked me and said they could not have done it without me, but what they meant was that they needed a neutral third person in the room to keep their discussions—and tone—on a positive track. Feel free to share this story if you ever need to assign a student to just observe rather than participate in a mediation role-play and if you'd like to explain how "less is more" in mediation.

Unlike these attorneys, during mediation, parties may decide against signing a settlement agreement. Instead, they may decide to go to trial, stay away from each other, or just live with the status quo. Sometimes, even if the parties cannot reach an agreement, the process of telling their story to a mediator and to the other side and feeling heard by both can make the dispute diminish or even disappear without need for a formal agreement.

When parties do reach an agreement, they decide what it includes. It may include simple solutions to the problem at hand: lights out at 11:00 p.m.; $575.50 to be paid by Aug. 29 at 5:00 p.m.; the plagiarizing student takes an online course in academic honesty and resubmits her paper; the barking chihuahua will be moved out of the apartment next door. Or, it may cover more expansive issues than the conflict seemed to present at the start and include creative win-win solutions that add value to both parties' lives. For example, rather than fighting about scarce parking and security, two neighboring businesses decide to join forces, share costs, and jointly advertise for new customers in ways that benefit them both. In another example, rather than evicting a senior citizen for hoarding, causing bad feelings among the tenants and possibly creating bad press, the landlord may provide a housecleaning and trash removal team to benefit all the tenants while increasing the value of the property.

Of course, win-win solutions can be reached during principled negotiation as well; the point here is that the mediators' role is to encourage the parties to work together to accomplish their goals with as little input from the mediators as possible.

For a sample mediation format for CRESL role-plays, see Chapter 3, "Sample CRESL Activities."

Online Dispute Resolution (ODR)

Today's students must learn how to negotiate and mediate in person, but they may be more comfortable negotiating by phone, text, or social media, and via online systems that are based on algorithms and artificial intelligence (such as those used by online sites to help buyers and sellers settle small disputes, regardless of where in the world they may be). **Online dispute resolution** (**ODR**), then, makes CR even more relevant and inviting to our students. For CRESL purposes, you can assign out-of-class ODR negotiation and mediation role-plays that mimic how these kinds of negotiations are done in business and legal settings worldwide.

2. CR and ESL: You Are Already Teaching Both

The Shared Pedagogy of CR and ESL

During my first years as an ESL instructor, I often caught myself planning lessons with anything and everything: Dear Abby, sitcoms, recipes, customer-service phone trees, radio call-in shows, and the kitchen sink. Finding authentic language experiences to engage my students "sparked joy" long before we had Marie Kondo to thank for that term.

This search for authentic ESL lessons became more interesting during my first CR training. I tried to focus on the content but was often distracted because the entire training seemed like a series of communicative activities designed for ESL purposes based on Vygotsky's (1986) collaborative, sociocultural approach. In other words, since CR is all about communication in pairs or groups, every activity seemed applicable to ESL, and the training overall felt familiar—almost like a content-based ESL course.

Here is a partial list of activities and approaches that are equally common in CR trainings and ESL classrooms: icebreakers, creating a classroom community, scaffolding, group work, teamwork, interviews, connecting content to students' personal lives, communicative competence, attention to culture and cross-cultural communication, critical thinking, student-centered approaches, experiential learning, peer feedback, language chunks, journals, accountability, assessment, reflective practice, and action research.

I hope that CR is starting to feel like "comprehensible input" (Krashen, 1985), just a little outside what you already know but as achievable as L +1.

The Role of Language In CR Training: Active Listening

Like ESL, CR has differing schools of thought and experts who disagree with each other, often collegially, in journals, panel discussions, and PowerPoint presentations. Within this range of approaches, *language* is a topic that may get a little or a lot of attention.

Most CR trainings teach the language of active listening, including the use of open-ended questions (*Can you tell us more about that?*); softeners (*And now we'd like to hear about your experience; would you be willing to tell us a little about that?)*; and reframing, one of the most powerful CR tools of all. Mediation professor and practitioner Ken Cloke (2013) gives these examples of reframing: Is he "lazy" or "relaxed"? Is she "bossy" or "a strong leader"? Did they not understand or did we not explain? Most CR trainings bring awareness to nonverbal communication as well, such as body language and the shape of the negotiation table, and to cross-cultural communication issues, both verbal and non-verbal.

For some CR professionals, language is practically the whole ball game, even when everyone is speaking English as their first language. Such trainings focus on specific words, grammar, pronunciation points, and syntax, all of which can create or prevent conflict—or promote peace.

For example, CR leader Marshall Rosenberg (2013), who titled his book *Nonviolent Communication: A Language of Life*, invites us to consider the effect of every single word: does it help or hurt? "Instead of being habitual, automatic reactions, our words become conscious responses based firmly on an awareness of what we are perceiving, feeling, and wanting. We are led to express ourselves with honesty and clarity, while simultaneously paying others a respectful and empathic attention" (p. 3).

As raising our students' awareness about word choices is already on our to-do list, why not do so in the ways Rosenberg suggests and give them lessons in both ESL and CR?

Let's consider how Rosenberg's advice plays out in real life. For example, when a mother encounters her teenage son's dirty socks in the living room again, Rosenberg suggests that the mother might respond this way: "Felix, when I see two balls of soiled socks under the coffee table and another three next to the TV, I feel irritated because I am needing more order in the rooms that we share in common. Would you be willing to put your socks in your room or in the washing machine?" (p. 6).

Although some of us might prefer to say, "Felix, get your socks out of the living room now!" it's worth considering the effect of *I* vs. *you*; the mother's focus on her own emotions rather than her son's bad behavior; and instead of a direct order, a choice of options in the form of a request to solve the problem.

In addition to this type of reframing, Cloke (2013) focuses on language in ways that could simultaneously give us a month's worth of ESL grammar lessons and bring more peace into the world:

- When considering pronouns: notice how *they* can lead to stereotyping and *we* can lead to partnership.
- In terms of verbs: notice the difference between *He is something* and *He did something*. Which holds out more promise for conflict prevention and resolution?
- For adverbs: do *never* and *always* express facts or feelings?
- In terms of syntax: note how this structure contributes to conflict: Pronoun + verb + accusation: *You are lazy*. Denial + pronoun + denial/ defense + counterattack: *No, I'm not, but you're a slob*. How can we reframe this conversation to state what's really going on? Cloke suggests that *You are lazy* could become *I need some help*.

The Role of Cultural Issues In CR Training

Like language, *culture* may get a lot of attention or short shrift in CR training. When it is included, the topics, often based on Geert Hofstede's (2001) work, would be quite familiar to ESL instructors: individualistic and collectivistic cultures, high- and low-context communication styles, long- or short-term orientations, formality and informality, and how all of these inform our students' learning and communication styles and entire world-views. Applying these concepts to CR raises interesting questions: How should we tell our conflict stories? How do we deal or not deal with emotions? Who should be at the table—just the parties themselves or the whole company, family, or neighborhood? If we reach an agreement, should we put it in writing or just shake hands? What is the role of apology and forgiveness in CR, and how should these be expressed and received? Can we lie? Will they lie? What is a lie?

Guidance for these last questions about lying is provided in Chapter 3, "Sample CRESL Activities," but for CRESL purposes, the standard answer to these types of questions is "It depends." You can explore what it depends on as much or as little as you wish.

Negotiation and Mediation in ESL: Double Meanings

In ESL contexts we often hear about *negotiating* meaning and *mediating* language learning. Michelle Kohler (2015) describes her study of three classroom teachers in Australia in *Teachers as mediators in the foreign language classroom*. And mediation is a key focus of the 2018 *Companion Volume with New Descriptors to the Common European Framework of Reference for Languages*

(CEFR) (Council of Europe 2018) because it can help address the "increasing linguistic and cultural diversity of our societies" (p. 22). But what does *mediation* mean in these contexts, and does it have anything to do with CR as discussed in Chapter 1, "Introduction to Conflict Resolution"?

Kohler (2015) uses *mediation* to describe what the ESL teacher does when "making sense of one language and culture for another" often through scaffolding, and what learners do on their own when moving between their first and target languages and cultures (p. 142).

The CEFR replaces the classic description of the four main language skills of *reading, writing, speaking,* and *listening,* with *reception, production, interaction,* and *mediation,* pointing out that *mediation* includes the other three. In the CEFR, *mediation* includes such ESL tasks as synthesizing meaning from various texts and adjusting register and tone for various audiences.

The *Companion Volume* has a strong focus on mediation in the sense of collaboration, teamwork, and problem-solving as key "soft skills" for 21st-century employment as well as for language learning. However, it does not seem to focus on training instructors or students to deploy these as mediation skills for the purpose of CR, even though CR is one of its descriptors for mediation.

Sometimes descriptions of mediation and negotiation for language and other purposes seem to apply just as clearly to CR even when not intended. One of CEFR's goals is to increase understanding, a goal shared by CR with similar and overlapping shades of meaning. And for ESL instructors who teach communicative competence, Peace Linguistics scholar Patricia Friedrich (2007) points out something that would be just as at home in *Getting to Yes* (Fisher et al., 2011): "All forms of interaction require negotiation" (p. 3). Kohler (2015) uses *mediation* to describe intercultural language teaching overall, with the teacher as a model of an "intercultural mediator" (p. 143) serving as "go-between" (p. 195) between the students' old and new languages and cultures.

Thus, Kohler's (2015) call for an "expanded" understanding of mediation for language learning purposes (p. 143) and the CEFR *Companion Volume*'s various uses of the term seem to support the propositions that ESL and CR are linked in many ways and that ESL instructors are already teaching CR to some extent, even if only indirectly, and could do so directly with a few tweaks to standard ESL activities. Some examples follow.

Icebreakers

When you start your class with an icebreaker, you are trying to build the kind of trust and rapport that are so essential to CR training and practice (see Chapter 3, "Sample CRESL Activities").

Grammar

ESL instructors routinely teach some version of the grammar points described earlier, such as pronouns, verbs, adverbs, modals, and syntax. With just a sentence or two, we can ask students to notice how *always* and *never*, for example, may contribute to conflict or promote peace.

Storytelling

Donna Tatsuki (2016), among others, has described the benefits of creating narratives for language learning, especially for vocabulary, grammar, speaking skills, overall academic development, and increasing empathy. If you use storytelling for any of these purposes, you are simultaneously preparing students to engage in CR activities, for there can be no conflict or resolution without stories. Negotiators must learn how to tell their stories and to listen to the stories of their counterparts. If they wish to reach a win-win solution, they must discover and create a third story on their own or with the help of a mediator.

If you include some kind of interactive component, such as an interview with the storyteller or peer responses to a story, you are already on your way to teaching active listening.

Role-Plays

ESL instructors often use role-plays to apply a vocabulary, grammar, or pronunciation lesson just learned in class to serve as a bridge to using it for authentic purposes both in and out of class.

We also use role-plays to improve communicative competence in general, as they demand careful listening and spontaneous but appropriate responses to unexpected information from others, the very same reason CR training depends on them so much. For CR role-plays, students can play themselves, a fictional or historical character, or an attorney or other representative of another person.

If you are already using role-plays, you are already prepared for the most effective way for students to learn and practice CR. For a detailed discussion of CRESL role-plays, see Chapter 3, "Sample CRESL Activities."

Academic Writing

How can teaching academic writing, regardless of the subject matter, promote a culture of conflict prevention and resolution? Consider the core values shared by these two very different endeavors: express our own voice and encourage others to share theirs; attend to one's audience; be clear; be fair; examine claims and provide evidence for them; include other writers' supporting and conflicting perspectives, and give them credit; include counterarguments; reflect; revise; use checklists; give and receive feedback.

In fact, giving and receiving feedback is necessarily an exercise in conflict prevention and possibly resolution as well. Whether in negotiation, mediation, or peer review sessions for writing, there are many ways to respond to statements besides agreeing or disagreeing. Examples include restating, clarifying, reframing, expanding, validating, questioning, inviting others to chime in, playing devil's advocate, and just listening without responding at all unless asked. In *Sharing and Responding*, a popular text on peer feedback used mostly in first language writing courses, authors Elbow and Belanoff (2000) describe 11 types of peer feedback responses, most of which work equally well in CR as effective responses to our negotiating counterparts.

For example, one of the most powerful techniques for both active listening and peer review in writing is to simply give the other person the opportunity to hear and reflect on their own thoughts without our helpful advice (Elbow & Belanoff, 2000). Thus, for both activities, standard responses include "Can you say more about that?", "Can you help me understand what you mean by x?", "Y sounds very important to you; is that right?" If you are teaching your students to use phrases like these during peer review in an academic writing class, you are also teaching them how to prevent and resolve conflict while protecting their relationships outside class. It would just take a sentence or two to point this out and invite writing students to try peer review-type responses with friends and relatives and to report back.

And, of course, this also applies to the feedback we ourselves provide to our writing students on the page and during writing conferences. We are probably already considering the options Ferris and Hedgcock (1998) describe, whether to be "directive," "nondirective," or "in-between" (p. 145). These happen to be the same options mediators and negotiators choose among to determine how to respond to parties. When we model effective uses of these options during writing conferences, we are simultaneously modeling the positive communication styles at the heart of CR.

There is one aspect of feedback that both CR and ESL could improve upon: Both fields focus on how to provide feedback, but what about how to receive it and respond to it? This topic is important to both fields and thus for CRESL, as well. Responding to feedback is the subject of another book from the Harvard Negotiation Project (see Stone & Heen, 2014).

The authors of *They say I say*, another popular writing text used mostly in first language courses, state that their approach "asks writers not simply to keep proving and reasserting what they already believe, but to stretch what they believe by putting it up against beliefs that differ, sometimes radically, from their own. In an increasingly diverse, global society, this ability to engage with the ideas of others is especially crucial to democratic citizenship" (Graff & Birkenstein, 2018, p. xxiii). Isn't this a beautiful description of both the writing process and principled CR?

With a deeper understanding of the connections between CR and ESL, my hope is that you feel ready to try some CRESL activities. I believe that these activities will seem familiar as ESL activities that, with a little tweaking, will help your students start preventing and resolving conflicts in English.

3. Sample CRESL Activities

How can you start providing CR training to your ESL students? Try some of the activities in this section, all of which were developed by my CRESL colleagues and me.

Building Rapport: Icebreakers

Both ESL instructors and CR practitioners know that the more rapport, trust, and goodwill, the better the communication process and the result. For negotiators and mediators in the United States, this may be two minutes of joint venting about traffic, parking, or the local sports team before getting down to business. Although this is often called *small talk*, and the amount of time devoted to it may indeed be small, the return on investment can be quite large, especially when participants use the conversation skillfully to create bonds and to transmit their hopes for a collaborative process and win-win solution. Note that in some cultures, it might only take two minutes to reach an agreement after many weeks, months, or years of relationship building.

For CRESL purposes, any icebreaker you already use will serve as double duty for rapport-building for CR, but here are some activities that work especially well for both:

- **Names:** Tell us your full name, what you like to be called, how to pronounce it, and how to remember it. Share a story or feeling about one of your names. Discuss this question: how can we prevent and resolve conflict just by addressing people according to their preferences?
- **Find someone who....:** Find one thing in common—the more surprising or obscure the better—with everyone in the class. What can we learn from this activity? How can we apply these lessons outside class to prevent and resolve conflict?
- **Concerns about the future:** In small groups, discuss your top three concerns about the future of the world and then compare lists with other groups. Reflect on the ways these discussions could help people build the kind of rapport needed to prevent and resolve conflict.

- **Conflict stories:** In small groups, discuss how conflict was handled during childhood at home and school, including on the playground. Tell at least one story about this from your personal experience. Report back to the whole class.
- **Goals:** Share your reasons for learning CR and your plans for using it in the future. Tell a story about this.

Introducing Conflict Styles: Arm Wrestling

CR trainings often start with an exploration of the five main conflict styles described in the Thomas-Kilmann (1974) Conflict Mode Instrument (TKI): *avoid, accommodate, compete, compromise,* and *collaborate* (see Figure 3.1). (Note that *cooperate* and *collaborate* are often used interchangeably in CR.) For CRESL purposes, these five styles can help students analyze their own conflict and communication styles as well as specific conflicts or conflict in general. These five styles can also provide a wealth of language activities, including lessons in vocabulary and idioms, word forms, pronunciation, and communicative activities such as group discussions and role-plays.

There are many ways to introduce the language and content needed to work with these conflict styles. One activity is the arm wrestle, a kinesthetic exercise that allows students to feel the physical sensations of the competitive and cooperative styles. Another approach is to start with the Conflict Styles chart (see Figure 3.1). I typically use the arm wrestle exercise as a lead-in to the chart.

The arm wrestle activity introduces students to two of the five conflict styles: *compete* and *cooperate.* Although there is certainly a time and place for skillful use of the competitive style, this activity leads students to the possibly counter-intuitive discovery that *cooperation* can produce results that are better than or equal to "winning." In other words, for purely selfish reasons, *cooperation* may sometimes be the best strategy if we want to "win." When we allow students to discover this for themselves, the results can be transformative.

Activity 1A: Instructions for Arm Wrestling

1. Announce
    - This is a completely silent exercise; no talking in any language.
    - If you do not want to do the exercise, that's fine; just observe.
    - Goal: Get as many points as you can.

2. Demonstrate
   - This is how you get a point. (Ask a student to demonstrate the exercise with you. From the arm wrestle position, allow the student to push your arm down. Then the student allows you to push their arm down.)
3. Give instructions
   - Without talking, find a partner.
   - Begin. Get as many points as you can; no talking!
4. Check in
   - After about 20 seconds, stop and ask how many points students have.

     Some students will have none; some will have many because they realized that by allowing each person to win a point, they could both get a lot of points.
   - State that everyone should have at least 10–15 points and ask them to try again.
   - If stuck, encourage students to look around the room at other pairs.
5. Reflect
   - What did you learn from this exercise? Did anything surprise you?
   - Describe any physical sensations you felt during this exercise. What does an impasse or a deadlock feel like? What does it feel like (in your body) to compete? What does it feel like to collaborate? Do you think you would have the same feelings in real negotiations?
   - What was the best way to get the most points? Why?
   - Is this always the best way to accomplish your goals? Why or why not?
   - Does this exercise remind you of anything in your own life? What about in current events, history, literature, or film? Use the idioms listed in Activity 1B to discuss your examples.
   - Does this exercise raise any cultural or cross-cultural issues? Why or why not?

Activity 1B: Language Lessons to Support the Arm Wrestling Activity: Word Forms

Complete the chart.

Verbs	**Nouns**	**Adjectives**
compete	compet _____	compet _____
collabor _____	collabor _____	collaborative

Activity 1C: Language Lessons to Support the Arm Wrestling Activity: Idioms

Match these idioms to the conflict styles you used in the arm wrestle exercise.

1. My way or the highway. ____________
2. Two heads are better than one. ____________
3. Win-win. ____________
4. Might makes right. ____________

Activity 1D: Language Lessons to Support the Arm Wrestling Activity: Role-Play

> <u>Instructions for students</u>: Choose a conflict style, but do not tell your partner which one you chose. Use your new idioms to "get your way."
> <u>Information for both partners</u>: You are in a crowded movie theater with no empty seats. You are seated in the center of a long row. The movie is starting.
> <u>Secret information for each party</u>: *Partner A*: The person sitting next to you, B, is yelling into a cell phone in a language you cannot understand, ruining the movie for your and your companion. *Partner B*: Your 90-year-old grandmother has just called to say that she is suddenly very sick and does not know what to do. You are struggling to communicate with her over the phone.

Activity 1E: Language Lessons to Support the Arm Wrestling Activity: Journal

Describe your experiences and three lessons learned during the arm wrestling activities. Use your new idioms and word forms.

Introducing Conflict Styles

Figure 3.1 is based on the Thomas-Kilmann (1974) Conflict Mode Instrument (TKI) described earlier. While working with this chart, students start seeing for themselves that there are many choices when it comes to dealing with conflict. Instructors, likewise, will see many opportunities to provide the language skills students need to explore these choices.

Figure 3.1 Conflict Styles Chart

Conflict Style	**Synonyms**	**Idioms**	**Communication Styles**
Avoid Pros: Cons: Examples:	*evade*	Don't rock the boat.	
Accommodate Pros: Cons: Examples:	*acquiesce*	Give in. Go with the flow.	
Compromise Pros: Cons: Examples:	*concede*	Split the difference. Half a loaf is better than none.	
Compete Pros: Cons: Examples:	*fight*	My way or the highway Take it or leave it. Jockey for position.	
Collaborate Pros: Cons: Examples:	*cooperate*	Two heads are better than one. Win-win situation.	

Source note: Contributors to this chart include Michael Clark, Melody Noll, and Jen Burton.

Some ways to use Figure 3.1 are listed.

- Discuss the pros/cons of each conflict style and give examples of skillful and unskillful uses of each one.
- Discuss similar terms and connotations in the students' first languages. Do any cultural issues arise concerning these terms? Focus on *compromise* and *collaborate.* Do these terms have any negative connotations? Do we all mean the same thing when we use these terms?
- Use the chart to analyze any conflict, real or fictional.

- Learn about the communication styles and language used for each style. Examples include *direct, indirect, aggressive, passive*, and *assertive* communication styles (Dale & Wolf, 2006).
- Reflect on the conflict styles we actually use (not the ones we think we use). Give examples.
- Consider the extent to which conflict is caused or prevented by conflict styles, regardless of the subject matter of the conflict.
- Explore conflict and communication styles in other cultures.
- Add the remaining conflict styles (*avoid, accommodate, compromise*) to the word forms chart in Activity 1B.
- Use Figure 3.1 to prepare outlines for presentations or essays on specific conflicts or conflict in general.

  Use Figure 3.1 for role-plays using various conflict styles and new idioms. Some role-play ideas are to put students in pairs and ask them to resolve disagreements using various combinations of conflict styles (e.g., compete vs. accommodate, or compromise vs. compete). Some sample disagreements are: (1) A is vegan; B loves BBQ; choose a restaurant. (2) A loves horror movies; B loves romantic comedies; choose a movie.

Understanding Conflict: Facts, Emotions, Needs, Solutions (FENS)

As we have seen, each conflict style has pros as well as cons, but the collaborative style is the one we use in CRESL to promote principled negotiation. As discussed earlier, principled negotiation takes us on a journey from the parties' demands (called *positions* in CR) to a new and deeper understanding of the situation based on the parties' emotions and needs, whether stated or unstated. *Needs* refers to the five categories in Maslow's hierarchy of needs (1943): *physiological, safety, belonging and love, esteem*, and *self-actualization.*

I created the FENS chart, shown in Figure 3.2, to help students organize and apply this approach in several ways. Students can use it to plan for upcoming role-plays and as a guide during any role-play that requires active listening, as shown in Activity 3A. During role-plays, students can use a FENS to keep track of new information and as a roadmap toward solutions. Outside of role-plays, students can use it as a framework for analyzing conflicts and as an outline for papers and presentations on various conflicts.

Even a simple analysis of an opposing party's emotions and needs can create a surprising degree of empathy and enthusiasm for seeking win-win solutions. You may recall the student who used a chart to analyze how World War I could have been prevented: she prepared FENS charts for Austria-Hungary, Serbia, Russia, Germany, France, and England to show how focusing on these nations' shared needs could have prevented that war.

Suggested activities follow the FENS chart (see Figure 3.2).

Activity 2A: Create a Class List of Common Emotions and Needs for CR Activities.

Examples are listed. Add idioms.

> EMOTIONS: sad, disheartened, heartbroken, glad, pleased, overjoyed, angry, indignant, livid, afraid, apprehensive, petrified, frustrated, annoyed, confused, bewildered
> NEEDS: survival, stability, safety, belonging, love, family, friendship, esteem, freedom, independence, control, respect, fulfilling one's duties, fairness, justice, harmony, honesty, nonviolence, equality, kindness, honor, self-actualization.

(Maslow, 1943)

Figure 3.2 FENS Chart

		Party #1	**Party #2**
F	**Facts** *Summarize the story from each participant's point of view.* *Check verb tenses.*	Position: Conflict style:	Position: Conflict style:
E	Emotions *Use adjectives and new idioms.*		
N	Needs *Use abstract nouns from Maslow's chart.*		
S	Solutions based on needs *Use modals for brainstorming.*		

Activity 2B: Assign a FENS

After your students become familiar with the FENS chart, you can simply assign a FENS to analyze any kind of conflict. One of my standard homework assignments is for students to watch a movie or TV show and then create a FENS for the characters involved in the main conflict. A variation is for students to create a FENS to analyze a current political or international conflict they read or hear about in news media. For a more personal assignment, students can prepare a FENS for anything that isn't going well in their lives.

For this assignment, students can create a FENS chart like the one in Figure 3.2 or they can create any configuration that makes sense to them. When analyzing more than one side of a conflict, it's useful to include a Venn diagram with space for emotions and needs that both parties share, and students often enjoy adding colors and shapes to help express their insights.

FENS charts pack in a lot of information for instructors, revealing patterns of understanding and misunderstanding, but are much easier to review than journals or essays. You can consider this a freewriting or journal exercise and address language points, as you wish.

Communicating to Prevent and Resolve Conflict: Active Listening Practice

Active listening is the communication skill that makes principled negotiation and mediation possible. As discussed earlier, its simplest form is to paraphrase and check whatever a speaker is trying to communicate. This serves two purposes at once: It allows listeners to make sure that they have understood the speakers correctly while showing the speakers that they (the listeners) are very interested in understanding what the speakers have to say. With the FENS chart as their guide, students can fulfill these goals not only with the facts the speaker is sharing but also with the speaker's stated or unstated emotions and needs. With this foundation, the participants can brainstorm sustainable solutions based on fulfilling the needs that have been identified.

I typically introduce students to active listening with the script in Activity 3A, but you may wish to start with a lesson or two on each step in the script, incorporating language lessons as needed (see Activity 3C for some ideas).

Note that active listening practice does not require a conflict. I usually start class on Mondays with an active listening activity in which students share their experiences from the weekend. Students can also use active listening to practice for job interviews. One student used active listening during her interview to join a sorority; the more she repeated back what the sisters were saying, the more they seemed to feel that she would be a perfect fit.

Note also that resistance to active listening is a common first reaction. Students often say that it isn't necessary because everyone heard what was just said, so why repeat it? Active listening could seem embarrassing, a waste of time, or even rude. Your responses could include:

- See how it feels when your partners provide you with active listening.
- Try your best, and afterward, we will ask your partners to tell you how they felt about receiving your active listening.
- This is what the Harvard Negotiation Project advises; this is what professional negotiators and mediators do in real life.
- Just try it in class to practice English.

Activity 3A: Active Listening Script

Scripts serve as training wheels to prevent students from veering off into other communication processes, such as chatting, venting, or advising. Scripts can also provide language chunks that students can memorize. Once students have internalized the purpose of a phrase, they can paraphrase it and make their own. You may wish to allow students to refer to lists of emotions and needs until they become familiar with these concepts and terms. The script also includes some blank spaces for students to fill in, on the spot, to start removing the training wheels.

Here are the instructions for using the script:

Instructors or students choose one of these topics or create their own: a current conflict, problem, or fear or something you wish others understood about your culture.

1. Assign Partners A and B.
2. Partner A (the first active listener) asks Partner B to respond to one of the questions. B has about three minutes to speak without interruption.
3. A takes 1–2 minutes to provide active listening to confirm and show understanding of the facts, emotions, and needs that B has shared or suggested. Or, A may use active listening to invite B to brainstorm possible solutions but A does not offer solutions unless B requests it.
5. Partners A and B thank each other and switch roles.

Sample Active Listening Script

A: Hello, I'm ________. What's your name?
B. Hello, ________. I'm ________. Nice to meet you.
A. Nice to meet you, too. Well, we're here to talk about ________. Can you tell me a little about that?
B: Yes, sure:

____

A: Okay, thank you. Let me make sure I understand what you're saying.

FACTS: I heard you say that ________________. Is that correct?
EMOTIONS: It sounds like you felt ________ and ________. Does that sound right?
NEEDS: What's important to you is ________ and ________. Have I understood you correctly? Would you like to say more about this?
SOLUTIONS (optional): Would you like to talk about some solutions? Just brainstorm any ideas that come to mind about how you could satisfy the needs we just talked about. After that, you can choose the best ones.
A & B: Thank you!

Example

After a few practice sessions, and a review of the reframing skills described in Chapter 2, "Conflict Resolution and ESL," active listening responses could sound like this:

1. Paraphrase and check the facts: *So, Andy, you are saying that you want to study at home on weekends, but you never know when your roommate Bob's friends will come over to watch sports and make a lot of noise. Have I understood you correctly? Is there anything you want to add?*
2. Validate the speaker's emotions, which may be stated or unstated: *Andy, it sounds like you are feeling angry, frustrated, and worried about your grades. Is that how you are feeling about the situation? Anything else?*
3. Explore the needs that may be causing such strong emotions and the conflict itself: *Andy, I noticed that you said you feel invaded when the weekend parties start. It sounds like having a secure home life is important to you, especially while you're experiencing culture shock,*

but you never know when you're going to feel kicked out of your own home. You also told us that you and Bob split the rent equally, but it feels like Bob is using the apartment more than 50 percent, which does not feel fair. You also mentioned that your parents spent a lot of money to send you here to study and that you feel a lot of pressure to get good grades so as not to disappoint them. And you told us that Bob was your only friend but you don't know if you can ever be friends again, and now you're lonelier than ever. And, neither one of you can move out, so you are stuck with each other for the next nine months.

So, to sum up, some important issues that you would like to resolve are: (1) finding a way to share the apartment in ways that are fair to both of you; (2) balancing your need to get good grades with your hope to have some kind of social life; and (3) trying to see if you and Bob can be friends or at least be on good terms for the next nine months. Does that sound about right? Do you want to add anything?

Activity 3B: Adding Active Listening Questions

With practice, students can add some standard but very productive questions to their active listening.

Examples:

- *I heard you say* home *(or another abstract noun). Could you tell us what you have in mind when you use that word? What does it mean to you?*
- *Can you repeat back what you heard ________ (the other side) say? I'm not asking you to agree with it, just to repeat it.*
- *If you could go back in time and change something that you did or didn't do or say, what would it be?*
- *How would you like things to be in the future, ideally?*
- *What do you need from the other party?*
- *Is there anything you would like to say or ask?*
- *Did you learn anything new here today?*

Questions like these can lead to apologies, forgiveness, and thanks, all great foundations for solutions or for the realization that it is not necessary to create specific solutions.

Activity 3C: Adding Language Lessons to Active Listening Activities

It's easy to add language lessons to active listening activities.

Verb tenses: Student A describes something from the past (a conflict, a scary childhood experience, or a historical event), the present (a troubling relationship or current event), or the future (an upcoming difficult decision or event). Student B paraphrases and checks to be sure they got it right. Focus on accurate use of verb tenses as you wish. Have students switch roles.

Question formation: Students practice with open-ended, closed, hypothetical, and rhetorical questions and responses. Example: *If you had known X, would that have changed anything? If you could have any solution you want, what would it be?*

Reported speech: *He said that she would refuse to pay the rent until the heater was repaired.*

Modals and other softeners: Raise awareness about *could, should, may, might, would, will,* and other ways to project politeness and openness.

Indirect and vague vs. direct and clear language: Raise awareness about the difference between being polite and being vague. Note the different language styles needed to brainstorm solutions (open) and to evaluate and write agreements that everyone can understand (clear and direct).

Vocabulary and idioms: Introduce words for emotions focusing on degrees of intensity for emotions such as anger (irritated to enraged) and colorful idioms (e.g., *You had steam coming out of your ears!*). This is usually a lot of fun.

For additional ways to integrate language points and CR, review Chapter 2, "Conflict Resolution and ESL."

Activity 3D: Creating Solutions

Creating solutions is a two-step process: First, we brainstorm possible options and then we evaluate them. You may wish to add a third step—writing up agreements—especially for negotiation and mediation role-plays, which are discussed later.

For brainstorming: the active listener lists all the needs the speakers have identified and asks them to brainstorm ways to satisfy those needs. Open-ended questions work best. Examples: *What are some fair ways to share the apartment? How could you and your roommate repair your relationship?* As with all brainstorming, all ideas are listed, no matter how unrealistic, because crazy ideas can lead to practical ones.

For any sort of problem you choose, ask students to generate a lot of ideas without the pressure of finding the right or best one. For example, my colleague Jen Burton gives each group a paper clip and asks them to brainstorm ways to use it.

1. Brainstorm at least 10–15 ideas.
   - Just generate ideas. Do not evaluate them.
   - Choose a recorder to write down every idea. It may help to write them on the blackboard.
   - Aim for quantity, not quality.
   - Be creative: crazy ideas can lead to good ones.
2. Evaluating options: to help speakers evaluate the solutions they just brainstormed, active listeners should ask them to answer questions from this checklist:
   - Does the solution meet the needs that the parties identified?
   - Is it realistic? (Will it work?)
   - Is it fair? (Does everyone have to do something?)
   - Is it specific? (Does it answer *who, what, when, where, why,* and *how?*)
   - Is it clear? (Can others understand it even if they didn't participate in the role-play?)
   - Is there a Plan B in case something goes wrong?
   - How could it be improved?

Active listeners ask (but do not answer) these questions, unless the speaker asks for help.

CRESL Role-Plays: Background Information for Instructors and Students

CR training focuses on role-plays: preparing for them, doing them, and then reflecting on them. Ideas and sources for role-plays are provided in Appendix A.

Whether the role-play is for active listening, negotiation, mediation, or conflict coaching (discussed later), it should allow students to experience lessons that they have covered or will cover in class or readings. Thus, some role-plays give students experience with various conflict styles or with the kind of active listening needed to deal with strong emotions or to learn new information about their partners, just as they would in jigsaw exercises as discussed earlier. More advanced role-plays create practical or ethical dilemmas for students to grapple with, such as deciding which information to disclose, balancing the need for a good relationship with the need to achieve a certain sum of money or other substantive goal, or finding the sweet spot between persuading and lying. CRESL instructors will immediately see that culture permeates all of these issues. They will also see opportunities to plant language lessons into any role-play.

For these teaching moments to occur as intended, students must understand how CR role- plays work, so I provide a handout based on these guidelines:

Role-play guidelines:

1. **Purpose:** The purpose of role-plays is for students to practice CR and English skills while learning about conflict, English, and themselves.
2. **Confidentiality:** Students should not share the confidential information they receive about their role with any other students, including those on the same side, without their instructor's permission.
3. **No outside research:** Students should not do any outside research on the issues in the role-play unless instructed to do so. If students point out that the role-play lacks certain crucial facts or includes something that would never happen in real life, they are probably right. However, role-plays prioritize CR lessons over reality and everything will work out as intended if they stick to the facts as given.
4. **Ethics:** Students should be given these instructions: *You may not change key facts or tell lies about things that are "material" (information your partner is relying on to make important decisions). However, you don't necessarily have to answer every question asked or reveal information that you feel that your character would not reveal. You may withhold information until you feel the time is right to share it. Exaggerating and persuading can be gray areas; sometimes*

permissible, sometimes not. These are excellent topics for reflections after the role-play.

5. **Before the role-play: Prepare!**
   a. Students should read their information sheet several times and note any words or ideas that are not clear. Students may get help from their instructor or possibly from a classmate with the same role.
   b. Students should know the facts by heart. It will help to practice answering these questions "in character": "What is this conflict about, from your point of view?" "What two or three things are most important to you in this situation?" "What information do you need from your negotiating partner?"
   c. Students should also anticipate language and pronunciation points that may arise. Which vocabulary words, idioms, and verb tenses will they need to tell their stories?
   d. Students should write a FENS for all the parties, including themselves. They should leave blank spaces where they are not sure about another party's information and then list the questions they need to ask to obtain it.
6. **During the role-play:**
   a. Students should keep their FENS in mind but should not just read aloud the emotions and needs they have listed. Instead, they should require their partners to try to discover this information through active listening.
   b. Students should remember that CR is voluntary, so their characters actually want to solve their problems even if they are angry or skeptical at first. Thus, students should not be impossibly or unbelievably competitive, but they should also not be too overeager or accommodating. Depending on the information about their role, they may show strong emotions, hopelessness, lack of trust, or personality defects, especially at the beginning, but they should not give their partners a hard time just for fun. Instead, they should respond, in character, to the new information and perspectives they gain through active listening. In other words, if they are engaged in skillful principled negotiation or mediation, their characters should evolve and end up in a better place than where they began.
   c. Students are not required to reach an agreement.

On the day of a role-play, CR instructors usually walk into class with stacks of handouts in two or three different colors, one for each party. Sometimes the handouts are pre-numbered so pairs of 1s, 2s, 3s, and so on simply find each other and get started.

However, for ESL purposes, it's better to start by giving parties on the same side an opportunity to discuss their roles together, noting any questions for the instructor. I send all the "greens" out into the hall to talk amongst themselves while I meet with the "blues." I will answer questions about vocabulary and clear up any confusion about the facts, but I will not answer any questions that students need to ask their green counterparts. Then the blues go into the hall, the greens return, ask their questions, and set up the chairs so that when the blues return, they can walk over to their partner and get started.

Students are often apprehensive before the first negotiation role-play, but once they get started, they often do not want to stop. They are intensely curious about the other side's confidential information and they are eager to see if they can solve the puzzle and create a win-win agreement, especially when it all seemed so hopeless at the start. Thus, it is important to tell students how much time they have to complete the role-play, write the timeline on the board, assign a timekeeper, and give at least a five-minute warning before time is up.

For the first few role-plays, I invite students to use the script in Activity 3A, the additional questions in Activity 3B, and their lists of emotions and needs. I always save at least five minutes after the role-play for closing, to give parties the opportunity to thank each other, ask for feedback, and to share their secret information and discuss what they could have done better now that all their cards on the table. Students are also asked to write reflections about their strengths and weaknesses, what they learned, what they want to work on, and what questions are on their minds. This can be done in class or for homework.

Role-Play Formats for Specific CR Processes

To apply the general background information to negotiation, mediation, or conflict coaching (discussed later), instructors should review the following role-play formats for each process.

Negotiation

There are hundreds of books, articles, websites, and videos about negotiation. The format presented here aims to summarize the main points needed for role-plays in CRESL classrooms.

Here's a checklist your students can use for classroom negotiations.

1. **Before the negotiation role-play:**
   a. Students should prepare as discussed earlier.
   b. Students should consider what they will do if they cannot reach an agreement with the other side. How could they get their needs met in other ways?
2. **During the role-play:**
   a. Students should start building rapport and trust during their first contact with the other side even if they are just arranging chairs or a time to meet. What message do they want to convey to the other side about the kind of negotiator they are? What if they are too nice and accommodating? What if they are too competitive even about small details?
   b. Students should start with some appropriate small talk before getting down to business.
   c. Students should transition from building rapport to focusing on housekeeping issues, such as creating a timeline for completing the role-play and creating a joint list of the issues they must address during the role-play. Example: "Well, I'm glad we had a chance to talk about X. Looks like we have a few things in common, and I hope that helps us have a good discussion and reach an outcome that works for both of us. I'd really like to hear how you see the situation, but first, should we talk about some 'housekeeping' issues?"
   d. Students should start telling their stories and actively listen to each other so that all parties have a chance to explain their perspectives and to ask and answer each other's questions. They should start with open-ended questions, just like they've done in active listening practice. It helps to remember these goals: understand how your partner sees the situation, find out what's really important to your partner, and help your partner understand the same things about you.
   e. After this general introduction, students should use their list of issues to ask and answer questions about these specific points. It

may help for them to imagine that they and their counterparts are on the same team, trying to solve a problem together, as they would do in any classroom jigsaw exercise.

f. Solutions (See Activity 3D) Additionally, students should consider trade-offs (*If he can do/give X, then I can do/give Y*). If students are asked to write their agreements, a good follow-up activity is to have them exchange agreements with other groups. Each group applies the checklist in Activity 3D to another group's agreement and provides feedback. Each group uses this feedback to revise their agreements.
g. Closing and reflections.

"Dirty Tricks"

Your students may be disappointed to see that our format does not include tactics to gain competitive advantages over their adversaries or to protect them from their adversaries' possible "dirty tricks," such as lying, evading, and making extreme demands. Despite all the earnest discussion about principled and collaborative approaches, when faced with an actual adversary during their first role-plays, students may want to have some tricks up their sleeves in case the other side uses a competitive style. We do have some tricks to offer, although they may not be what your students have in mind. Here are the strategies, based on ideas from *Getting to yes* (Fisher et al., 2011), I give my students to help them see how to protect themselves against "dirty tricks":

Strategy #1: Prepare, as discussed.

Strategy #2: Be sure to have a Plan B in case you cannot reach an agreement. A bad deal can be worse than no deal, and reaching agreement is not required.

Strategy #3: Trust but verify. If you are worried that you cannot trust the other side to tell you the truth, you are right—you can't. It's *your* job to get the information you need; it's not their job to hand it over to you.

Strategy #4: Can you agree to disagree? Can you reach a good agreement even if you are sure the other side is lying about something? If you find yourself stuck in a never-ending argument, stop and consider whether or not you and your partner can still resolve the conflict even if you disagree about whether certain statements are true or false.

Strategy #5: Do you need outside help? If you and your partner are stuck, is it because someone else needs to be at the negotiation table? Are you lacking certain information and perspectives? How can you solve these kinds of problems?
Strategy #6: If you can see that your partners are using some kind of dirty trick, stop negotiating, say that you can see what is going on, and suggest a break. When you come back, explain your approach to negotiation and ask how they would like to proceed. If the answer is not satisfactory, you can thank them and say goodbye, knowing that you have other alternatives.

Mediation

There are probably just as many books, manuals, websites, and videos about mediation as there are about negotiation. There are also community mediation trainings open to the general public; these usually take 30–40 hours to complete. Real-life mediations may take anywhere from 30 minutes to several days, but generally last about 2–4 hours.

What does mediation look like? Picture an active listening exercise with three people: the mediator and two parties. The mediator starts by asking Party A to tell their story, responds with active listening, and then turns to Party B for the same exercise. For the first few role-plays, mediators could use the script in Activity 3A for both parties and then turn to some of the questions in Activity 3B.

In real life, mediations may take place with one, two, or three mediators, and with two or more parties. Before the mediation, mediators may receive a great deal of information about the dispute, or very little or none at all.

For CRESL purposes, I use one or two mediators and two parties unless the numbers don't work out, in which case I'll use three parties before resorting to three mediators. The mediators receive no information about the dispute, which provides an authentic need to apply their active listening skills. While I meet with the parties as discussed earlier, the mediators meet with their co-mediators to decide who will handle which parts of the mediation; how they will deal with breaks; and what they might do if the parties get stuck, etc. This is called a *briefing*. I meet with the mediators last so that they are in the classroom to set up the chairs and welcome the parties back from the hallway into the mediation space they have created. I encourage mediators to sit near the blackboard so that they can make FENS charts in real time for all to see.

The format presented here is a very general summary of the mediation process, but it works well for CRESL classroom purposes. For a three-minute video overview of a CRESL mediation, see www.mslmediation.com

1. Mediators welcome the parties.
2. Introductions: Mediators should ask how the parties wish to be addressed and parties should respond in character; mediators use their own real names.
3. Opening:
   a. Mediators explain their roles (they are there to help the parties talk to each other, not to decide who's right or wrong, or what they should do).
   b. Mediators explain the process and may suggest ground rules, such as not interrupting or no name calling.
4. Storytelling and active listening
   a. The mediator asks Party A to tell their story to the mediators (not to Party B, who will benefit from listening to the exchange between the mediators and Party A). The mediator responds with active listening and then repeats the exercise with Party B. The mediator tries to give each party the same amount of time and attention.
   b. After the initial round, the mediator uses some of the questions in Activity 3B.
   c. The mediator may invite the parties to ask each other questions, using active listening.
5. Seeking solutions
   The parties start seeking solutions using Activity 3D. The mediator's roles are to
   - Facilitate brainstorming using active listening without making suggestions unless asked.
   - Keep notes on the proposed solutions.
   - Use the checklist to help the parties evaluate and select solutions.
   Optional: The parties may write and sign an agreement.
6. Closing: Everyone thanks each other and says goodbye.
7. Reflections: Mediators ask for feedback, and parties may ask each other questions. Participants write reflections on lessons learned during class or for homework.

Conflict Coaching

Conflict coaching is a CR process used when only one party, the client, seeks help from a mediator (coach). The other party may be unwilling or unable to participate, or the client may just prefer to meet with the coach alone. For CRESL purposes, this is an excellent process to use when mediation is too complicated to set up, when you'd like students to work in pairs, or when you'd like to focus on interviewing skills.

Here are the steps for a simple conflict coaching role-play (based on Amadei, 2011).

1. The coach and client build rapport.
2. The coach describes the process.
3. The client identifies goals for conflict coaching.
4. The client tells their story. The coach responds with active listening and provides other perspectives for the client to consider.
5. The coach invites the client to brainstorms options and to select the best ones.
6. The coach and client may rehearse conversations with the other party.
7. The coach and client discuss any next steps.

4. CRESL Applications

Now that you know more about CRESL, how can you adapt it for your classroom? Think back to the activity described in the Introduction that involved asking students to choose a conflict and then work with classmates to resolve it. Are you ready to try it, perhaps through active listening, negotiation, or mediation? If not, are you ready to ask students to analyze a conflict with the conflict styles or FENS charts? If not, how about a simple active listening exercise based on students' experiences, a story you are reading in class, or a current event?

To help you take one or more of these steps, this section offers design tips for creating your own CRESL activities along with some sample lesson plans, a list of CRESL applications to a wide range of academic skills and content areas, and questions to help you reflect on CRESL applications for your particular teaching purposes.

Design Tips for CRESL Activities

Integrated CRESL activities should include several of these features:

- CR content
- CR communication skills
- ESL skills that are in sync with CR goals
- Role-plays and other activities to practice and apply CRESL skills to authentic situations
- Critical thinking: Did the CR method work? Why or why not? What adaptations should be made for individual or cultural variations?
- Reflections: Students should reflect on these questions: What have I learned? What do I want to practice? What do I want to explore? What went well? What could be improved?

Sample lessons applying these design tips are listed.

1. *Conflict and Communications Styles*

CR content: There are five main conflict styles: avoid, accommodate, compromise, compete, collaborate. Each one has pros and cons depending on the situation. For each style, give an example of its use from current events or history and explain whether the use was skillful or unskillful.
CR communication skills: There are three main communication styles: aggressive, passive, and assertive (or "appropriate"). Practice matching the communication and conflict styles by observing them in the media and by acting them out in simple role-plays.
ESL skills: Introduce idioms and word forms for each conflict style. Focus on sentence structure, direct/indirect language, modals, and pronunciation (stress, intonation) for each communication style.
Role-plays: Using the conflict and communication styles and new ESL skills, work with partners to prevent and resolve various fictional and real conflicts.
Critical thinking: Would conflict and communication styles work the same way among people in your home country/culture? How would these have to be changed? Are there more than five ways to deal with conflict? Propose at least one additional style to add to the chart.
Reflections: Which styles were most effective/most comfortable for you as a speaker and as a listener? How would you like to improve your communication skills for conflict prevention and resolution? List two or three takeaway lessons that you will practice next time.

2. *Active Listening*

CR content: The keys to preventing and resolving conflict are empathy and skillful communication. Information is power, especially when it comes to learning about the other side's true interests, needs, and values, despite what he/she may be demanding. Practice analyzing conflicts with FENS charts to learn what to actively listen for as a negotiator or mediator. Examples: practice with movies, friends, and real-life encounters.
CR communication and ESL skills: Learn and practice how to ask various types of questions; develop a repertoire of skillful verbal and non-verbal responses (nodding, eye contact, backchannels,

paraphrasing, clarifying, reflecting, reframing, summarizing, apologizing); and respond to expressed and unexpressed emotions.

Role-plays: Practice with active listening scripts until students can engage in active listening on their own. An example would be: *In a role-play in which one party is filled with rage, can the student adapt the linear order of facts, emotions, and needs to the situation by starting with emotions and needs, and then reframe the facts so that the party feels understood? Can two negotiators use active listening to brainstorm solutions, evaluate them, and then select the best ones? Can mediators use active listening to help parties work together to brainstorm, evaluate, and select solutions?*

Critical thinking: In what ways could active listening help to prevent and resolve conflict? How would it have to be adapted for your culture or for your personal preferences?

Reflections: What is comfortable/uncomfortable for you about active listening, as the speaker/listener? What do you need to work on?

CRESL Applications to Academic Skills and Content Areas

Some of the many ways that CR can be used in lessons to improve academic skills are listed. (Jen Burton contributed to these ideas.)

Academic Skills

- Use active listening to lead and participate in group discussions.
- Give an individual or group presentation on CR topics. Use a FENS chart to anticipate your audience's needs. Use CR language skills to help your audience understand you.
- Choose common conflicts among students for analysis and role-plays. Examples are graded group projects, social media problems, classmates asking each other for help, and roommate issues.
- Choose common conflicts among instructors and students for analysis and role-plays. Examples are plagiarism, absences and late arrivals, late papers, and email and office hour etiquette.
- Develop relationships with buddy CR or ESL instructors on your campus or around the world. Create online role-plays and other activities for students in both classrooms.

All-Purpose Assignments for Any Content Area

- Provide daily or weekly active listening practice to make this skill second nature.
- Assign conflict styles or FENS charts to analyze and outline conflicts for role-plays, presentations, or papers.
- Use online dispute resolution (ODR) to prevent and resolve real or fictional conflict in and out of class. As discussed earlier, ODR uses email, text, chat, Skype, etc., and can be synchronous (everyone is communicating at the same time) or asynchronous. With transcripts, recordings, or video, these authentic communication activities can enrich language lessons in grammar, vocabulary, pronunciation, etc.

Literature

- Identify and analyze the conflict styles of main characters.
- Make FENS charts for the main conflicts. Propose alternative endings based on the characters' emotions and needs.
- Analyze the characters' language and communication styles and propose alternative dialogue that would prevent conflict and promote peace.
- Use active listening, negotiation, or mediation role-plays to explore and resolve conflicts between the characters. Try to reach win-win agreements.
- For an excellent description of these CRESL applications to literature, see Marcus, *Literature in ELT: Using literature for conflict resolution* (2015).

History

- Identify and analyze the conflict styles used in historical conflicts. Propose alternatives that might have produced better outcomes.
- Choose a war. Use a FENS chart to analyze and try to prevent it.
- Negotiate or mediate conflicts between powerful and powerless people in history.
- Mediate between Alexander Hamilton and Aaron Burr right before they duel.

Science and Technology

- Select current hot topics: the environment, gene splicing, self-driving cars, social media, artificial intelligence, or using algorithms in criminal justice. Use FENS charts and active listening role-plays to seek understanding about various points of view. Compare this approach to the customary debates on these topics.
- Animal behavior/ethology: research and report on CR among animals.
- Archaeology and anthropology: research and report on CR among early humans.
- Game theory: research "prisoner's dilemma"; the British game show, "Golden Balls"; and other applications of game theory to CR. Create new computer games to test principled CR against competitive methods.
- Video games: explore various methods of CR in video games. Create a video game with alternative endings based on the CR method selected.

Medicine

- Role-plays
    - A doctor and patient use active listening to discuss the patient's disease.
    - Various parties (parents, doctor, insurance carrier, hospital administrator) must decide whether a terminally ill child should be kept on life support.
    - An experienced nurse disagrees with a new doctor about ordering a procedure.
- Interview patient advocates or ombuds about how they prevent and resolve conflict.

Business

- Practice job interview skills using active listening.
- Use active listening to role-play customer service scenarios, such as customers complaining about a product or service or businesses interviewing customers about their needs for products or services.
- Role-play a contract negotiation using principled negotiation.

- Supplement business case study assignments with an exploration of potential conflicts.
- Research and report on ODR programs for eBay, Airbnb, and similar businesses. Choose a business and design your own ODR process for it.
- Research "systems design" for conflict management in large organizations. Choose a business and design its conflict management system.
- Learn about college competitions for business negotiations and create or join a team. One example is the Intercollegiate Negotiation Competition held in Tokyo: http://www.negocom.jp/eng/.

Law

- Students use active listening to role-play attorney-client interviews.
- Select a classic U.S. Supreme Court case with a 5–4 decision. Students prepare a FENS chart to analyze the various opinions and explore other possible approaches to the dispute.
- Select a case that students have briefed or that is used for moot court or trial practice. Students negotiate or mediate the case and compare their results to the actual outcomes.
- Students conduct principled negotiations from start to finish outside class using phone, email, Skype, chat, document sharing, and other ODR methods.
- Students research court Alternative Dispute Resolution (ADR) requirements and options in your jurisdiction. How would they include ADR in their litigation plan?
- Students interview local mediators. Ask permission to observe a mediation.
- Review www.mediate.com. Read articles, mediator profiles, training descriptions, etc.
- Students visit a small claims court and note how conflicts are resolved.
- Students research collaborative law, and analyze the pros and cons.

Criminal Justice and Law Enforcement

- Analyze the conflict styles in the movie/play *Twelve Angry Men*. Make a FENS chart for all twelve jurors.

- Research restorative justice for criminal law and school discipline. Invite guest speakers.
- Research and role-play hostage negotiations.
- Research community policing in your community. Invite guest speakers.
- Research how complaints against police are handled in your community.

See if there is a mediation program and, if so, invite guest speakers.

Social Justice

- Students select hot topics of keen interest to research, analyze, and role-play.
  For example, use active listening to interview real or role-played parties affected by homelessness; make FENS charts for homeless people, advocates, merchants, residents, and police; and conduct a multi-party mediation to try to resolve a specific problem related to homelessness, such as opposition to emergency shelters in various neighborhoods. Examples of other social justice topics for multi-party CR role-plays or analysis are environmental justice, immigration, due process in sexual harassment cases, and cultural and religious conflicts.
- Students analyze and reflect on how violence and non-violence are presented in popular culture.
- Students analyze the most effective ways to communicate about social justice issues.
- Students research and participate in "Dialogue" programs, in person or online. Dialogue programs provide opportunities for structured communications among people who differ based on backgrounds and beliefs. Their goal is to increase understanding and possibly seek common ground. Internet searches for "intergroup dialogue" will provide examples.
- Instructors can explore the TESOL committees and publications on social justice, English for Peaceful Purposes, Peace Linguistics, and intercultural communication.

Global CR/International Relations

- Model United Nations: research, role-play, and participate.
- United Nations: research the CR programs and methods it uses. Propose improvements.
- Diplomacy: research, invite guest speakers, and role-play.
- Choose a region that is experiencing significant conflict. Research efforts to promote peace and understanding in that region. Examples may be the United States Institute of Peace, Mediators Without Borders, Witness for Peace, Nonviolent Peaceforce, Women in Black, and similar organizations. Invite guest speakers. Use negotiation or mediation role-plays to explore solutions based on understanding the needs of all sides.
- "Peace Camps": research, participate, and create your own.
- Research and report on efforts to connect young people from conflict zones through sports and music. Brainstorm new programs to accomplish the same goals.
- Research and report on museums related to war and to peace. Create a peace or CR-related museum.
- Write a national anthem that promotes empathy, interdependence, and peace.

Academic Reading and Writing

CR makes a fine theme for an academic reading and writing unit or whole course. There is plenty to read on the topic itself and on specific types of conflict in just about every discipline in the humanities and social sciences. Violence versus non-violence and war and peace are always provocative topics. For rhetorical analyses, there are frameworks to follow and challenge, such as the step-by-step process in the book *Getting to Yes* (Fisher et al., 2011). For experiential learning, role-plays can be used to explore various arguments and counterarguments in readings and essays. Restorative justice (RJ), with its applications to school discipline and criminal justice, is particularly interesting to students, and persuasive essays on using RJ or the traditional criminal justice system in specific cases provides plenty to discuss, summarize, paraphrase, quote, write, counter-argue, and conclude.

How Can You Provide CR Training in Your ESL Classroom?

Here are some questions to help you apply the information in this ebook to your own classroom.

1. In what ways are CR basics already part of your ESL classes?
2. Describe three CRESL activities you could use for your current teaching purposes.
3. Imagine that you are asked to create a CRESL course for your campus or department. Describe the course you would love to create.
4. Connecting with campus resources: Which offices, programs, and/or courses on your campus already address CR? Consider ombuds, peer mediation, campus dialogue, peace and conflict studies, business communications, and career planning. Could these programs provide guest speakers or training for you or your students? Are these programs accessible/welcoming to ESL students? What new CR programs/courses could benefit ESL students on your campus?
5. Connecting with off-campus resources: does your community have community mediation centers? If so, could they provide guest speakers or training for you or your students?
6. Describe any obstacles you might face when trying to use CRESL activities or when trying to propose a new CRESL course. How could you overcome them?

Concluding Thoughts

I hope you have found some personal and ESL connections to CR and are excited about trying a few CRESL activities in your classroom. And I hope you have identified some support for doing so on your campus, in your community, or at least in Appendix A.

Your feedback about the ideas in this book would be welcome and appreciated, as would thoughts about needs for training or additional materials. Please send feedback to the author at bj.roberts@yahoo.com

Appendix A
Next Steps and Resources for Instructors

The information presented in this ebook should be enough to introduce your students to basic CRESL activities, but here are some easy ways to build on that foundation.

1. Background reading
   - *Getting to Yes* (Fisher et al., 2011)
   - *The Language of Peace: Communicating to Create Harmony* (Oxford, 2013)
   - *Mediation: Empowerment in Conflict Management, 3rd Edition* (Domenici & Littlejohn, 2020)
   - *The Compassionate Classroom: Relationship Based Teaching and Learning* (Hart & Hodson, 2003)
2. Additional CR activities and role-plays
   - U.S. Institute for Peace: https://www.usip.org/public-education/educators/peacebuilding-toolkit-educators-high-school-edition
   - Conflict Resolution Education (CRE): https://creducation.net/
   - Peer mediation training for high school students: https://communityboards.org/youth-schools/publications/
   - *A World of Fiction* (Marcus & Berman, 2014): This collection of short stories for ESL students includes ESL activities for each story. Once students work through the stories and activities, they will be ready to apply your choice of CR lessons to the conflicts and characters.
   - Teaching materials from the Harvard Negotiation Project (although these must be adapted for ESL purposes): https://www.pon.harvard.edu/store/.
   - Radio or television call-in talk shows
   - The daily news; comments sections in online news websites
   - Student proposals

3. Mediation training
    - CRESL courses for international ESL students: UC-Berkeley Summer English Language Studies (http://summerenglish.berkeley.edu); look for Conflict Resolution and Alternative Dispute Resolution.
    - CRESL training for ESL instructors: Please contact the author: bj.roberts@yahoo.com.
    - Check for community mediation organizations in your community like https://communityboards.org/.
4. Websites
    - mediation.com
    - mslmediation.com
    - https://www.campus-adr.org/

Appendix B
Commonly Asked Questions about Teaching CRESL

Throughout my 15-plus years of giving CRESL presentations, ESL instructors have taken to CR like ducks to water. But during breaks and as I'm packing up, the instructors who most want to try CRESL have shared these confessions and concerns. My responses are based on my experiences as a mediation student, mediator, and CRESL instructor.

1. *I don't enjoy dealing with conflict; I'm not good at it and I'm actually afraid to face it. Can an avoider like me still teach CRESL?*
   Yes, indeed, and you are not alone! Here are some tips for avoiders:
   - Remember that you don't actually have to negotiate or mediate any conflicts while teaching CR. In terms of content, CR is just another topic to analyze like any other subject. In terms of communication skills, think of the material as expanding on things you are already teaching, such as asking for clarification; participating in a group; providing peer feedback; and offering and supporting jigsaws, interviews, and dialogues. Expect students to carry out your assignments as ESL activities as usual. They may not be any more afraid of CR than anything else we ask them to do, and they will probably enjoy it more than other activities.
   - Start with something non-threatening like the Conflict Styles chart. Once your students start discussing examples, role-plays will be a natural next step, because role-plays start with introductions and "paraphrase and check," two bread-and-butter ESL activities. When it comes to negotiation, I hope the discussion about *principled negotiation* lowered some anxiety at least for CRESL purposes. Nobody wants to risk embarrassment or blowing up a relationship. But is it really that scary to set up a role-play in which Student A asks Student B some questions about how she sees the situation

and what's important to her and then asks if she'd be interested in hearing how Student A sees things?
- The best way to get over fears is to learn more, especially by reading *Getting to Yes* (Fisher et al., 2011). Or, take a look at one of author William Ury's YouTube videos. Find an online or live mediation training. Check out other videos of children and teens performing peer mediation.

2. *What if students are uncomfortable with some of the material, such as emotions, and feel that CR activities are too personal? What if they say that CR sounds like therapy. Is it?*

   No, CR isn't therapy, but it may be therapeutic.

   CR and ESL share the values of student empowerment and safe classroom communities, so do not insist that students participate in any particular activity or share anything that they consider too personal. Instead, thank them for their feedback and turn this into critical-thinking and ESL exercises by asking questions like these: How would the conflict be handled within their own cultures? How would they suggest dealing with emotions that may come up during real or role-played conflict with people from a variety of cultures? Which vocabulary and idioms do their first languages use to describe emotions, and how do these compare to similar terms in English? Additionally, students can always observe CR activities until they become more comfortable participating in them, and they can be encouraged to write down reflections that they will not be asked to share with classmates or instructors. Having said all that, after a few role-plays, my students quickly see that emotions permeate conflict and appreciate having the FENS chart and active listening tools to address them.

3. *What could go wrong?*

   The answers are the same in the ESL classroom and in real life during actual negotiations and mediations:

   - Failing to reach an agreement is not failure. Did the students try to apply the framework? Did they listen to each other, learn something new about the conflict or themselves, consider options for resolution, and leave on good terms with the other party? In real-life CR, we call this "making progress." Fisher and colleagues (2011) put it this way: "The process is the product" (p. 30). Thus, CR works even if the parties just listen and try to understand each other. Whether or not students reach an agreement, we debrief to analyze what was and was not accomplished; reaching or not reaching an agreement can be equally valuable outcomes depending on the lessons we learn from them.

- Getting stuck—a.k.a. *impasse*—is another common feature of real-life CR. Many books, articles, and workshops help mediators and negotiators think about and deal with it. Can the impasse be overcome by taking a break; offering additional money; or learning more about the other person's needs, hobbies, or family? These are just a few tricks of the trade. One surprising piece of advice about dealing with impasse is to be transparent about what's going on. A mediator might say to the parties, "Looks like we're stuck. I'm not sure what we should do right now. Who has an idea?" A negotiator might say, "I think we've been going around and around on the amount of back rent. How about we agree to disagree on this for now, go get a cup of coffee and talk about another issue, maybe the barking dog?" But the impasse may also turn out to be the end of the road. If so, what will the parties do instead of reaching agreement? Are these options better than agreeing to a bad deal? Again, failure to overcome an impasse is not failure. Ending the session and then having a frank discussion with one's counterparts about what was going on and what could have been done differently can be just as valuable as solving the problem.
- What if students get into a real disagreement during a CR role-play? In CR, everything is grist for the mill. Anything that happens can turn into a lesson to achieve better outcomes in the future. And most problems have the same solutions: being transparent (i.e., naming what's going on), asking the parties (i.e., your students) to suggest what needs to be done, and then reminding them to apply active listening. If an activity works the way you hope it does, great! Now analyze what went well. If an activity goes down in flames, also great, but analyze what didn't go well and what can be done differently next time. (I'm pretty sure I'm already supposed to be doing something like this for all of my ESL lessons, right?)

4. *What if I tried to apply CR for classroom management and didn't like the result?*

Join the club. CR takes training and experience and still does not always work out the way we hope. But when you and your students have a common language of CR, you have the opportunity to use the failure as a learning experience: Be transparent. Ask students what's going on and what could be done better. Apply the conflict styles and

FENS charts to this real-life classroom situation. To practice standing in another person's shoes, you can turn the situation into a negotiation or mediation role-play in which students take turns playing the instructor.

5. *What if students insist that interest-based CR is too weak to stand up to human nature? We're animals, after all.*
   First, as discussed earlier, students are asked to try this method, not to believe in it. And have they actually tried it before raising these objections?
   Second, you can play "the Harvard card"—you are teaching the approach that was developed and taught there, and *Getting to Yes* (Fisher et al., 2011) is full of examples of how this approach works very well indeed in diplomacy, business, and our daily lives, if the participants are sincere and skillful.
   Third, this is a great opportunity to explore beliefs vs. facts about animal and human nature. Primatologist and ethologist Frans De Waal's 2016 book, *Are We Smart Enough to Know How Smart Animals Are?* includes his observations of elderly female chimpanzees who "step in" when males fail to reconcile after a fight (pp. 184–185). The female chimp positions herself in a certain way, grooms one male chimp and then the other, and then leaves them to complete the job of making up. De Waal describes this as "mediation," and many professional mediators would agree that this sums up their job. De Waal also reports on the everyday cooperative and tension-reducing actions common in chimp colonies expressed through grooming and food sharing. He does not call this "negotiation," but I don't think he would object. It's not that conflict and physical power plays don't arise among chimpanzees because they certainly do, but according to De Waal, chimpanzees have developed ways to resolve their conflicts, and it's rarely through bloodshed. So, if chimps are our closest animal relatives (is 98.6 percent shared DNA close enough?) does that change the meaning of "We're animals, after all?"
   But what about all the bloodshed in human history? There is no denying it, but what about all the small and large ways we have also found to prevent and resolve it? Humans have been cooperating, negotiating, mediating, and otherwise preventing and resolving conflicts every single day for thousands of years, so why don't we consider "peacemaking" our inherent human nature? After all, don't we eventually end our wars, usually with peace treaties?

This fascinating topic is beyond the scope of this book, of course, but it may be an excellent one for your teaching purposes or general interest. If so, you might consider Ury (2000) or Wright (2001); both provide compelling evidence that human nature is the very reason principled negotiation and mediation are so effective, and probably our only hope.

6. *But does principled CR always work?*
   No. Sometimes conflicts can only be resolved by compromise, flipping a coin, divorce, walking away, trial, legislation, competitive bargaining, civil disobedience, DNA evidence, agreeing to disagree, giving in, giving a gift, or an act of violence. And some conflicts may never be resolved. However, even when principled CR does not solve the problem in a tangible way, what benefits may result from trying it first?

Appendix C
Sample Syllabi

For a discussion of four types of CRESL courses (academic skills, IEP, academic reading and writing, and negotiations for LLM students/attorneys), see Roberts (2018).

Syllabi for the first two courses described in that article are provided here:

Conflict Management for Academic Success at the University, College Writing (CW) 21

Course Description:

This 3-unit course is for international and other students who are new to UC-Berkeley or to any American university. Students will learn and practice cross-cultural communication strategies to help them fully participate in academic life. Using conflict resolution (negotiation and mediation) as the substantive course theme, students will develop strategies for resolving communication problems, misunderstandings, and conflicts that can arise in academic settings and beyond. This course also helps students improve academic and class participation skills, including understanding lectures and instructions; contributing to and leading group discussions; speaking up in class; participating in group projects; public speaking; critical thinking, reading, and writing; "academic honesty"; attending office hours; asking for and using feedback; and understanding the use of American humor in the classroom.

Classroom activities will require authentic university-level language and thinking and will include learning the language and terms of art for conflict resolution and the university classroom; developing frameworks for analyzing conflicts and negotiation strategies; negotiation and mediation role-play simulations; active-listening exercises; group discussions in which students agree/disagree with each other; individual and group presentations; and lectures, note-taking, and question-and-answer sessions.

Thus, with conflict resolution as our focus, our classroom will serve as a laboratory for practicing the types of communication, classroom participation, and critical and creative thinking that your professors and classmates will expect from you at UC-Berkeley.

Required Texts:
Fisher, Ury, Patton, *Getting to Yes* (3rd. ed. 2011) Penguin Books (GTY)
Course Reader

Course Grade:

15%: Class participation (in-class group work & whole class interactive lectures)
20%: Individual presentations
15%: Homework & journals
5%: Lead a group discussion
5%: Office hours and emails to instructor
20% Group Presentation Project: Getting to Yes
20% Negotiation or mediation project

A sample syllabus for a short multi-skill IEP course with a CR theme follows.

Conflict Resolution Communication Skills

Course Description:

This course is an intensive introduction to Alternative Dispute Resolution (ADR) for international students with intermediate-advanced ESL skills. ADR includes negotiation, mediation, arbitration, and other ways to resolve disputes without court trials or violence. We will apply ADR to conflicts involving business, culture, law, international relations, the environment, and our personal experiences. We will also explore conflict resolution in our various cultures and across cultures.

This course is "two for the price of one": students will improve their English while learning practical conflict resolution skills with people from different cultures. Our focus on negotiation and mediation role-plays will help students achieve more confidence and natural fluency in English for academic and professional purposes. Thus, in this intensive course, you will develop practical skills to resolve personal and professional conflicts and avoid culture clash, enhance your fluency, and acquire strategies for improving your reading, writing, listening comprehension, and conversation skills.

Required Texts:
Course Reader
Getting to Yes, Roger Fisher, William Ury, & Bruce Patton (Penguin Books, 2011)

Grades:
This course may be taken Pass/No Pass or for a letter grade.

25% Reading & writing assignments and quizzes
50% Participation in role-plays and class exercises
25% Final project

REFERENCES

Amadei, R. (2011, March). Conflict coaching. Retrieved from https://www.mediate.com/articles/AmadeiR1.cfm

Cloke, K. (2013). *The dance of opposites: Explorations in mediation, dialogue and conflict resolution systems design.* Dallas, TX: Goodmedia Press.

Council of Europe (2018) *Companion Volume with New Descriptors to the Common European Framework of Reference for Languages (CEFR).* https://www.researchgate.net/publication/338178234_Council_of_Europe_2018_Common_European_Framework_of_Reference_for_Languages_Learning_Teaching_Assessment_Companion_Volume_with_New_Descriptors_Strasbourg_Council_of_Europe_Publishing_Authors_B_North_E

Dale, P., & Wolf, J.C. (2006). *Speech communication made simple* (3rd ed.). White Plains, NY: Pearson Education, Inc.

De Waal, F. (2016). *Are we smart enough to know how smart animals are?* New York: W.W. Norton & Company.

Domenici, K., Littlejohn, S. W., and H. Ricci (2020). *Mediation: Empowerment in conflict management, 3rd Edition.* Prospect Heights, IL: Waveland Press, Inc.

Elbow, P., & Belanoff, P. (2000). *Sharing and responding* (3rd ed.). New York: McGraw-Hill.

Ferris, D., & Hedgcock, J. (1998). *Teaching ESL composition: Purpose, process, and practice.* Mahwah, NJ: Lawrence Erlbaum Associates.

Fisher, R., Ury, W., & Patton, B. (2011). *Getting to yes: Negotiating agreement without giving in* (3rd ed.). New York: Penguin Books.

Friedrich, P. (2007). *Language, negotiation and peace: The use of English in conflict resolution.* New York: Continuum.

Graff, G., & Birkenstein, C. (2018). *They say I say: The moves that matter in academic writing* (4th ed.). New York: W.W. Norton & Co.

Hart, S., & Hodson V. K. (2003). *The compassionate classroom: Relationship based teaching and learning.* La Crescenta, CA: Center for Nonviolent Communication.

Hofstede, G. (2001). *Culture's consequences: Comparing values, behaviors, institutions, and organizations across nations* (2nd ed.). Thousand Oaks, CA: Sage.

Kohler, M. (2015). *Teachers as mediators in the foreign language classroom.* Bristol, England: Multilingual Matters.

Krashen, S. D. (1985). *The input hypothesis: Issues and implications.* New York: Longman.

Marcus, S. (2015). *Literature in ELT: Using literature for conflict resolution* http://blog.tesol.org/literature-in-elt-using-literature-for-conflict-resolution/

Marcus, S., & Berman, D. (2014). *A world of fiction: Timeless short stories.* White Plains, NY: Pearson.

Maslow, A. H. (1943). A theory of human motivation. *Psychological Review, 50*(4), 370–396.

Oxford, R. L. (2013). *The language of peace: Communicating to create harmony.* Charlotte, NC: Information Age Publishing.

Roberts, B. J. (2018). Using *Getting to Yes* to teach English, negotiation and other 21st century skills. *Journal of Research Institute, 58*, 7–93.

Rosenberg, M. B. (2013). *Nonviolent communication: A language of life* (2nd ed.). Encinitas, CA: PuddleDancer Press.

Stone, D., & Heen, S. (2014). *Thanks for the feedback: The science and art of receiving feedback well.* New York: Viking.

Tatsuki, D. (2016). How to teach narratives: A survey of approaches. *Journal of Research Institute, 54*, 5–29.

Thomas, K. W., & Kilmann, R. H. (1974). *Thomas-Kilmann conflict modes.* Tuxedo, NY: XICAM.

Ury, W. (2000). *The third side: Why we fight and how we can stop.* New York: Penguin.

Vygotsky, L. (1986 [1962]). *Thought and language.* (A. Kozulin, Trans. & Ed.). Cambridge, MA: MIT Press.

Wright, R. (2001). *Nonzero: The logic of human destiny.* New York: Vintage Books.